MY DOLPHIN LIFE

by Shoshana Stopek
illustrated by Jesga Machado

PICTURE WINDOW BOOKS
a capstone imprint

Published by Picture Window Books,
an imprint of Capstone
1710 Roe Crest Drive
North Mankato, Minnesota 56003
capstonepub.com

Library of Congress Cataloging-in-Publication Data is available on the Library of Congress website.
ISBN: 9798875239335 (hardcover)
ISBN: 9798875239281 (paperback)
ISBN: 9798875239298 (ebook PDF)

Summary: Follow a dolphin through her day as she finds food, plays with friends, feeds her calf, and stays safe.

Editorial Credits
Editor: Christianne Jones
Designer: Kay Fraser
Production Specialist: Whitney Schaefer

Printed and bound in China. PO 6461

Hello there! I'm a supersmart bottlenose dolphin. I live in the beautiful blue ocean. The temperature is nice and warm—just how I like it.

I live with a group of dolphins. Do you know what a group of dolphins is called?

A pod! Dolphin pods are made up of males and females. Pods can have as few as two or as many as 50 dolphins!

From hunting to swimming, we do
everything together.

Dolphins talk to each other through clicks and whistles. It's our own secret language. Sometimes it's like we're telling jokes!

Speaking of talking, it's time for whistle practice with my calf. Every calf develops a signature whistle early in life.

The whistle acts as the dolphin's name. It's how dolphins recognize each other.

I love playing with my friends. Check out my powerful jump! *WHOOSH!*

Do you think my tail or my flippers help me jump so high?

I use all my body's strength to jump, but *especially* my tail. I use my tail flukes to paddle and move through the water.

I use my flippers to steer. I can do some fancy tricks like a gymnast!

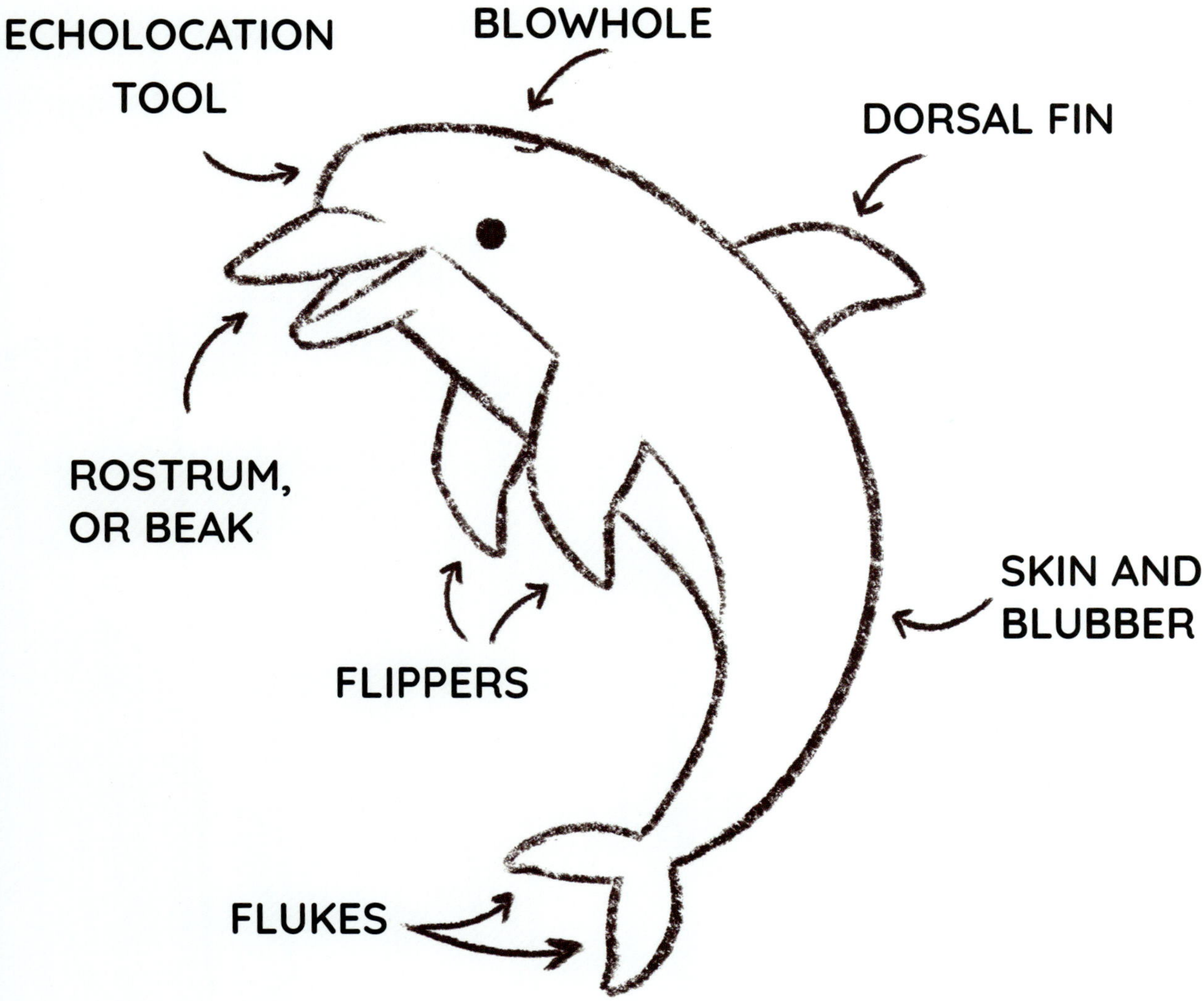

ECHOLOCATION TOOL

BLOWHOLE

DORSAL FIN

ROSTRUM, OR BEAK

SKIN AND BLUBBER

FLIPPERS

FLUKES

It's time to nurse my calf. She's three months old. When she's six months old, I'll teach her how to fish.

Right now I'm teaching my calf how to breathe from her blowhole. We practice a lot.

The pod is hungry. It's time to hunt. We gather in a big group and take off! I keep my calf close and swim in the middle of the pod to protect her.

We feed a few times a day and eat fish, squid, and crustaceans.

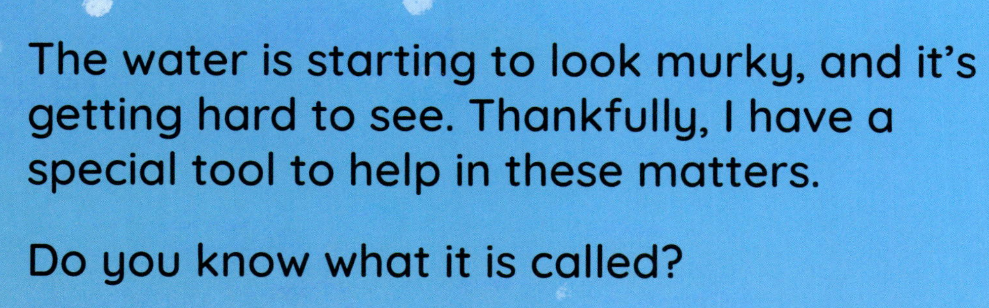

The water is starting to look murky, and it's getting hard to see. Thankfully, I have a special tool to help in these matters.

Do you know what it is called?

It’s my echolocation tool! This tool lets me “see” with my ears. It helps dolphins find and track food. It also helps us communicate and alerts us to danger.

Listen. Did you hear that? It could be a tasty treat hiding. Let’s check it out!

This is how echolocation works. I make high frequency clicking sounds. The sounds bounce back to me when they hit something. It's like playing a game of Marco Polo.

1 A dolphin sends out clicks from its blowhole.

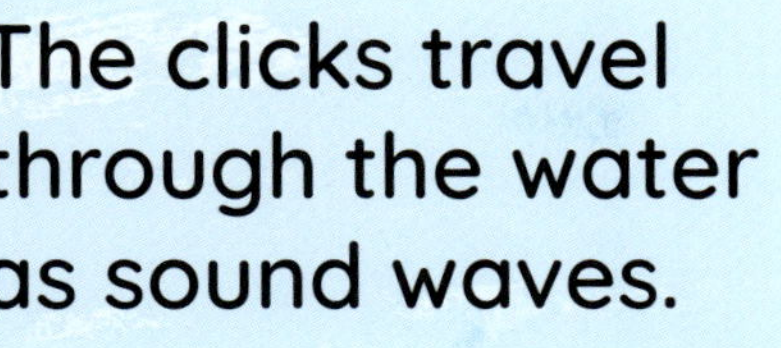

2 The clicks travel through the water as sound waves.

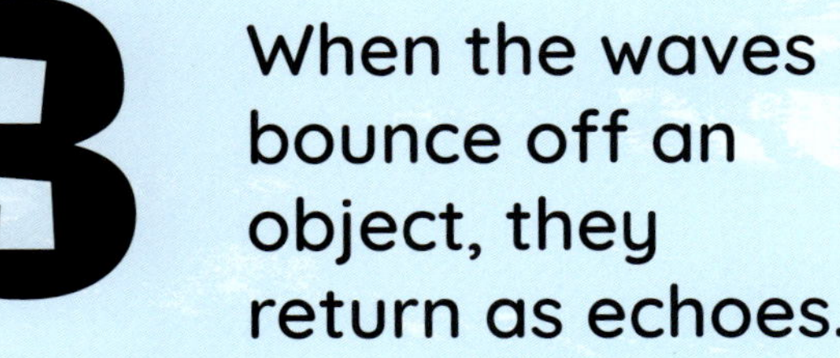

3 When the waves bounce off an object, they return as echoes.

4 The echoes help the dolphin “see” the size, shape, and position of objects around them.

Aha! It *was* a tasty treat! A little snack for me. But the pod still needs to eat.

Look at that giant school of mackerel near the coral. We rush back to the pod.

Using our signature whistles,
we discuss our plan.

Should we sneak up quietly
or rush in fast?

WHOOSH! We rush in and surround the mackerel. Lunchtime!

Sometimes, we see strange things floating in the water. These items look like food to us.

Should we eat them or leave them alone?

Leave them alone! That isn't food. Trash can make me and other dolphins sick. We need clean water to stay healthy and happy.

You can help us by keeping the beaches and oceans clean.

We keep swimming, staying alert. The ocean is full of danger, like sharks. I see one up ahead!

We protect each other by sticking together. There's safety in numbers. And sharks usually leave us alone if they don't feel threatened.

After a full day, it's time to wind down and sleep under the stars. I cuddle close to my calf. I sleep with one eye open to always keep us safe.

Thanks for spending the day with me!

Dazzling Dolphin Facts

- Dolphins are warm-blooded mammals, just like humans.
- There are more than 40 different species of dolphins. Dolphins come in many different shapes, sizes, and colors.
- Bottlenose dolphins are the most popular type of dolphin. They are known for being highly intelligent and very friendly.
- A dolphin calf stays with its mother until it is three years old.
- Dolphins have hair when they are born. It falls out shortly after birth.
- Dolphins sleep with one eye open because only half of their brain sleeps at a time. The other half stays awake to watch for danger.

Glossary

blowhole (BLOH-hohl)—a hole on top of a dolphin's head through which it breathes air

calf (KAF)—a baby dolphin

crustacean (kruh-STEY-shuhn)—an animal with a hard shell, jointed legs, and antennae who lives mostly in water; includes creatures such as crabs, lobsters, shrimp, and barnacles

echolocation (ek-oh-loh-KAY-shuhn)—a special skill dolphins use to "see" with sound by sending out clicks and listening for echoes

fluke (FLOOK)—the flat, paddle-like part of a dolphin's tail that helps it swim fast

high frequency (HI FREE-kwuhn-see)—sounds that move at very high speed; for dolphins, very fast sound waves that move so fast they are undetectable by humans

mammal (MAM-uhl)—a warm-blooded animal that breathes air and produces milk for its baby

pod (POD)—a group of dolphins that lives and travels together

school (SKOOL)—a big group of sea animals swimming together, like fish or dolphins

About the Author

Shoshana Stopek is the author of numerous books for all ages, including *Cows Wear Polka Dots* and *Hammock for Two*. She writes books that inspire curiosity, compassion, and connection. When she's not writing, Shoshana works in the entertainment industry and enjoys life in Los Angeles with her family. Visit her at shoshanastopek.com.

About the Illustrator

Jesga Machado graduated with a degree in computer science, but quit her programming career in 2015 to pursue her dream of becoming an illustrator. Since then, she has created artwork for textbooks, picture books, magazines, and board games for clients worldwide. Jesga also created the "Ano do Amigo" project, which produced and sold table calendars for six years to raise funds for an animal shelter in Brazil. Jesga lives in Sorocaba, a city in São Paulo, Brazil.